Becoming a Lake Girl and Family

Owning and Operating a Family Resort on The Magical Lake of the Ozarks

DEBRA AMANDOLA

Copyright © 2021 Debra Amandola.

All rights reserved. No part of this book may be used or reproduced by any means, graphic, electronic, or mechanical, including photocopying, recording, taping or by any information storage retrieval system without the written permission of the author except in the case of brief quotations embodied in critical articles and reviews.

Balboa Press books may be ordered through booksellers or by contacting:

Balboa Press
A Division of Hay House
1663 Liberty Drive
Bloomington, IN 47403
www.balboapress.com
844-682-1282

Because of the dynamic nature of the Internet, any web addresses or links contained in this book may have changed since publication and may no longer be valid. The views expressed in this work are solely those of the author and do not necessarily reflect the views of the publisher, and the publisher hereby disclaims any responsibility for them.

The author of this book does not dispense medical advice or prescribe the use of any technique as a form of treatment for physical, emotional, or medical problems without the advice of a physician, either directly or indirectly. The intent of the author is only to offer information of a general nature to help you in your quest for emotional and spiritual well-being. In the event you use any of the information in this book for yourself, which is your constitutional right, the author and the publisher assume no responsibility for your actions.

Any people depicted in stock imagery provided by Getty Images are models, and such images are being used for illustrative purposes only. Certain stock imagery © Getty Images.

Print information available on the last page.

ISBN: 978-1-9822-7341-5 (sc)
ISBN: 978-1-9822-7340-8 (hc)
ISBN: 978-1-9822-7339-2 (e)

Library of Congress Control Number: 2021917589

Balboa Press rev. date: 11/02/2021

Dedicated to my children and their children:

Erik, Kerstn, Jaxon, Vincent and Maya

Contents

Introduction ix

Chapter 1: Our Early Years at the Lake 1
Chapter 2: Transitioning to the Lake in 1959:
 The Big Decision 7
Chapter 3: Sacrifices for the Move to the Lake 15
Chapter 4: Moving to the Lake: The Adventure Begins 18
Chapter 5: Developing the Resort: Settling into Lake Life 36
Chapter 6: Enjoying Our Life 47
Chapter 7: The Last Three Years in the Resort 56
Chapter 8: Transition Out of the Resort and
 Lake Girl Qualities 71
Chapter 9: Lake Girl for Life 83
Chapter 10: Lake Challenges 88

Appendix 1: Facts about the Lake of the Ozarks 91
Appendix 2 97

Introduction

The winds of change were upon us as a small family as we moved from the city to the Lake of the Ozarks in central Missouri. This family was my family, Bob and Bette Christenson, and me, Debra Christenson Amandola. It was January 1960, and it was the snowiest winter on record. The memories of those times shaped me in ways I never would have expected, cementing my future and my very being. In this book, you will hear many stories about how my family became lake people and thereby created a lake girl in me. I have so strongly become a lake girl that I had to make my children and grandchildren lake people also.

The Lake of the Ozarks is located in central Missouri, about equal distance (between 170 and 180 miles) between

Kansas City and St. Louis. It is owned by Ameren, Missouri, and was created in 1931 when the power company (Union Electric) created Bagnell Dam on the Osage River. The dam was completed in February 1931, and the lake began generating power in May 1931. It covers fifty-four thousand acres and is more than ninety-two miles long. It has been recognized as a premier vacation destination in Middle America and has been voted as the Best Recreational Lake by readers of *USA Today 10Best*. (*St. Louis Post Dispatch*, April 12, 2016).

Chapter 1 will provide the big picture of my parents' transition to the lake, including elements of my childhood, and introduce you to us as a family who became strong lake people. You will also be introduced to my parents' positive parenting and our family structure.

Chapter 2 will introduce you to Bob and Bette and what contributed to their decision to move to the lake. The move was based on a typical decision many try to make as they move from working for a company to becoming self-employed. Also, Bob and Bette faced adversity as children, and you will hear briefly about how each of them overcame this and intentionally created a positive and constructive life and family. You will also learn more about me, who was five years old at the time of the move. The business that the family bought and moved will also be introduced.

Chapter 3 gives a perspective on what was given up with this change in location and business. This includes social aspects, financial hurdles, and educational prospects. All of this depicts that when you make a choice for one thing, you make a choice to sacrifice others.

Chapter 4 describes the adventure of the first couple of years at the lake. This covers the time frame of January 1960 to January 1962. During this time, Bob left his previous employer, we adjusted to lake life, some of our friends and family visited, tragedy struck, I started new activities, we made new friends, and Bette became very involved in the Camdenton, Missouri, school district. Bob's dad, my grandfather, moved in with us when he retired from working for forty-two years. The first two years were an adventure.

Chapter 5 covers the years 1962–1965, when we all settled into the operation and lake life. We started cooperating with other businesses for advertising, built the resort, had some fun, settled into school and winter activities, and began dreaming about other improvements and things we wanted. This was an exciting time for us with new friends, new challenges, and new school involvement for both Bette and me.

Chapter 6 takes us into a new place, encompassing everything at the resort and our personal lives. The years between 1965 and 1969 brought new things, such as a new kiddie pool, newly renovated cabins, more repeat business, and opportunities to provide a part of the business that helped me work toward a goal I wanted. We also started vacationing during the holidays. We all settled into roles and responsibilities to make the business run more effectively.

Chapter 7 describes the enhancements we made to the resort, our lives, and how we created more of what we wanted. I was able to sell minnows and use the profits to buy a horse. Bob built a new, larger cabin and a pool and enlarged and remodeled our house. We started vacationing in Florida over the holidays. During the years between 1969 and 1972, we created a very successful operation and found our workload actually decreased and our enjoyment increased. In May 1972, I graduated from Camdenton High School, and then Bob and Bette listed the resort to sell it.

Chapter 8 walks through the family's transition. This shift helped Bob and Bette increase their presence at the lake. I went away to college, and Grandad followed Bob and Bette. The years from 1973–1989 were full of activity for all and brought many lake-related accomplishments. All of us have reflected on what this experience has taught us. Specifically, I have reflected on what I have developed through this experience to become a lake girl.

Chapter 9 describes what I have done to continue to invest in my lake girl qualities as an adult. This includes investing my time at the lake. I have intentionally created the same qualities and values with my children and grandchildren. After traveling all over the world, I made the decision that the lake is a very special and unique place. This understanding was influenced by my perception of water safety, cycles of the lake, my customer values with people, and the ability to live in the now.

Chapter 10 is the final chapter, and I will describe what I think the lake means to my family going forward. I will also describe the challenges the lake itself faces to be sustainable for one hundred or more years in the future.

The first appendix provides facts about the Lake of the Ozarks area. The second appendix is a letter I wrote to my father.

Chapter 1

OUR EARLY YEARS AT THE LAKE

Our journey at the lake led to significant changes in our lives. We moved from the Kansas City area to the rural area of Lake of the Ozarks in central Missouri. I saw this change as an adventure. There were so many new things to explore and learn. We also left many family members and friends in the city. Our lives became much more rural—shockingly so. For the first few years after our move, my father stayed with the airline company where he had worked for more than eighteen years, coming home for the weekends to the lake. This helped mitigate the financial risks by not cutting off our income right away. I had just begun kindergarten in the city, and there was no kindergarten in the local school, which had three grades per room. Yet, I had the great outdoors to explore, and it taught me about the water, reptiles, and ducks.

Our social life was enhanced with several things in the first three months. My mother's sister, who was disabled with one leg and a prosthesis for the other leg, came with us as a companion to my mom and me. In the first seventy days in this new environment, there was a big opportunity. My dad had tickets for us to fly from New York to California on one of the first transcontinental flights for TWA airlines. We first needed to get to Kansas City (160 miles), and then we would travel by air to either coast. He was super motivated to do this. After February 1, 1960, and during the next sixty days, the lake area received more than sixty inches of snow. We were snowed in at the resort at the lake. My dad parked at the top of our road (about one mile of hills and curves) and walked down to our house. He connected a ladder to our tractor and used it to bring the luggage and us up the hill. While we waited at the top of the hill in the car, my dad took the tractor back and walked up the hills to get to us. We did make the trip, and it was more fun than we'd even thought it would be. This motivation and ingenuity were how we moved through our lives at the lake.

More about what drove these changes and the strategies we used to mitigate them can be read in chapter 2. Our social life was enhanced further when my paternal grandfather moved in with us when he retired from working for Santa Fe Railroad for forty-two years. He was then sixty-five, and I was seven. He became the fourth (Aunt Ann had moved out) member of our family and worked with us to create a beautiful resort.

He did odd jobs around the resort, such as sweep the sidewalks and patios and help garden. He was also my playmate, as we did many things together, such as fishing and playing games and eating sardines and other fish. He loved this from his Swedish youth. My grandfather also provided financial support. This money significantly improved the resort. His transition into our small group was typical to any addition to any team. This will be explored more fully later.

My childhood was full of amazing, unique, fun, and educational experiences. My parents raised me with positive parenting. Two examples have stayed with me. When I was three, I painted my dad's red car with the white paint that was opened next to it. He was not happy, yet he asked me to ask for help next time and took responsibility for the mishap because he'd left the open can of paint so close to the car. The second (also when I was three) was the time my dad purchased a stuffed skunk for me at the airport in Wichita and I lost it. He asked a flight attendant who was going to Wichita to get another stuffed skunk for me, and he surprised me with it one day. I still have that skunk on my dresser today.

My experiences at the lake were unlimited and varied. They ranged from learning to water-ski at age five to playing with reptiles, helping around the resort, and buying a horse myself. All of these formed the foundation for me to become a lake girl. My parents provided me challenges and rules commensurate with my age and maturity. The examples of positive parenting are extremely relevant for many generations to come.

My education at the lake started at Hurricane Deck Elementary School in the Camdenton, Missouri school district, which had three rooms for eight grades. My class included sixteen children who went to school together for seven years.

My mother became involved in the county bond issue to improve schools as well as the local PTA, and within a couple of years, the school was expanded. I was so proud that my mom had become significantly involved in the school and community effort to improve the schools in the Camdenton, Missouri, district.

With my mother's help, I became involved in a local Lutheran Church of America (LCA) Kent Memorial Lutheran Church in Sunrise Beach, Missouri, and attended Sunday school and vacation Bible school consistently for years. My mother's involvement in both education and church helped me tremendously. I think my mother was a big fish in a little pond, and she found ways to have a huge impact on the world around her.

The years from 1960 to 1973 had changed all of our lives. When my parents sold the resort, they became real estate agents, and this completely changed their lives from a resort-owning-and-operating family to real estate agents. This was now the third career for each of them, and you will hear more about this in the next two chapters. I was off to college and my adult life. When my parents told me the resort had sold the first weekend they visited me at college, I experienced bittersweet feelings I had never felt before. I was relieved I could do anything I wanted, yet I knew I would miss the resort and all the fun we had there. I wondered what life would be like. I was so curious about what my parents would do, as I had four years of college in front of me. Little did I know what would happen. I so enjoyed coming home during college to see my family and watch the lake and my parents evolve, as most places do over thirty years. Now that I look back, it was my opportunity to create lake people in my family: my husband, children, and grandchildren, as well as some friends. It was as an adult that I became appreciative of the lake and all it had given me.

Chapter 2
TRANSITIONING TO THE LAKE IN 1959: THE BIG DECISION

My parents, Bob and Bette, met in 1946 in the Kansas City area. Both had adversity in their childhoods. Bob was working at the Kansas City Airport for Transworld Airlines as the primary person overseeing everything that went in and out of the airport. Bette was working as a cashier at the Uptown Theater in the Valentine neighborhood of Kansas City. They married in April 1948 at age twenty-four. They intentionally decided to have a positive life going forward.

Bob and Bette Christenson

Bette's childhood years were spent in Coldwater, Kansas, in the southwestern part of the state. She was the third of eight children, and they lived on a farm before eventually moving into town. The older children helped provide childcare for the younger children. In 1938, when she was fourteen, her parents divorced. Her father moved barrels of oil, and he had invented and held the patent for a work dolly at that point. The divorce hurt him financially and emotionally, and he relocated. My maternal grandmother remarried shortly thereafter.

At this time, my mom started having grand mal seizures, and everyone was perplexed. Her mom was busy with a new marriage and several small children, and her sister Edith, my mom's aunt, stepped in to help her with this health challenge. The Mayo Clinic diagnosed my mother with epilepsy.

My mother and Aunt Edith left with a treatment plan, which included Dilantin and phenobarbital. She would take this medication for the rest of her life. She was able to drive because her seizures were 100 percent controlled. After my mom graduated from high school, she moved to Wichita and then to Kansas City. She was twenty-two when she met my dad.

Bob's life began in La Junta, Colorado, in 1924. His brother, Jerry, was born just two years later. When my dad was four and Jerry two, their parents divorced, and Bob and Jerry moved with their mother to Topeka, Kansas, to stay with her parents. Every year they took the train to La Junta to spend a two-week vacation with their dad, who worked for Santa Fe Railroad.

When my dad was eight, and he lit a match in a barrel to see what was in it, and it was gasoline. He was burned, and this scared their grandparents, as you can well imagine. Shortly after, Bob and Jerry's grandmother died, and their grandfather told my dad that Bob's burns caused the stress that caused her death. Shortly thereafter, the boys moved to Kansas City and lived with their mother.

It was now the depression of the 1930s. My dad told me that when he was twelve, his mother married a man who did not like him. That was all he told me, and I could tell it was tough for him. When he and Jerry were teenagers, they rode the bus around Kansas City and then started riding their bicycles around the metropolis. Both of them attended Central High School. In February 1941, they came home from school, and their entire family was at their apartment to tell them their mother had died in a car accident. My dad was a senior in high school, and Jerry was fifteen. Each was cared for by an aunt. My dad went to live with Aunt Lisa in Merriam, Kansas, (a suburb of Kansas City), and she had four children. My dad slept in a bed on the screened-in porch from February until he graduated from high school. Jerry went to live with Aunt Anna who lived in Topeka, Kansas, with no children.

Dad's father encouraged him to go to college, and he was off to Boulder, Colorado. He was seventeen and not ready for college, so he came back to Kansas City. He started working for TWA at this point. In 1942, he enlisted in the US Navy, and when they asked about his skills, he mentioned the airport experience he had, and they shipped him to the airport in Honolulu, Hawaii. Finally, he had some luck in his life. He spent the next two to three years working at the Honolulu airport through the US Navy. Considering what was happening in the rest of the world, he was lucky. This experience showed him there was a good world out there and his negative experiences were nothing compared to the goodness. He came home with a new lease on life. At this time, my Hawaii-educated father went back to work for TWA at the Kansas City airport. His experience in Honolulu gave him additional skills to use for TWA, so he firmed up his career in airport management. Shortly after he came back to Kansas City, he met my mom.

When they were married, they committed to live a positive and affirmative life going forward. They bought a house, got a dog, and went about living their life in the Kansas City area. My mom started working in an office with several other women, and they became good friends for the long term. My parents did not think they could have children and started building a new house. Both of my parents told me that I was their miracle child, and when my mom was pregnant, she did not take her medication. They were living in a third-floor apartment just east of the Country Club Plaza when I was born in October 1954.

When I was just a few months old, my mom had a seizure and then started taking her medication again and never stopped. She kept her epilepsy super quiet. When I was less than a year old, we moved to the new house my dad was building. I can remember parties at the house and them dancing and enjoying life. My dad ended up building one more house, and we moved to it when I was two. When we moved to this house, I reacted by not doing my appropriate toilet training business. My mom told me if I would start doing this in the bathroom like I had been, they would put up the swing set at the new house. It did not take long for me to get my act together because I wanted the swing set working. My mom tied what I wanted to something she wanted, and this worked.

We made great friends in this house and did a lot of entertaining with neighbors and family. I remember days spent going to the swimming pool and celebrating holidays with our extended family at our house. My parents planted a Colorado blue spruce tree at the corner of the yard for my third birthday, and it is now about thirty feet tall.

Before we moved in 1960, we sold the house my dad built and moved to a ranch house in Roeland Park, Kansas. I made a very good friend there, and we started kindergarten together at Rosedale Elementary School in the Shawnee Mission School District. By the time we moved to the lake, I had lived in four places. It was this that prepared me for the move to the lake because of the new friends and positives in each change.

It was this fall when my parents decided to move to the lake and bought a resort. They told me that my dad was feeling some frustration totally outside of his control at work, as young people with college degrees were being promoted over him. He knew his future with TWA was not what he wanted for the next few years. With their house builds and sales, they accumulated a nice down payment to put toward the resort. They both wanted a future they had control over and the rewards that followed their hard work. The resort and fishing camp they bought was named Shangri-La Resort, located off State Road F in the Sunrise Beach, Missouri, area. This resort was on the

25-mile marker of the Osage Main Channel of the Lake of the Ozarks in the back of a mile-long cove. The resort was built in the 1930s as a fishing camp. It had four stone cabins, a four-plex of large studio units, and a single cabin for two. The dock was in disrepair, and the entire resort needed updating. These are pictures of the rental units in 1960.

Pictures of the rental units in 1960.

Chapter 3

SACRIFICES FOR THE MOVE TO THE LAKE

*E*very time a choice is made for something, a choice is made to sacrifice something. By making the decision to relocate us to the Lake of the Ozarks in January 1960, several things were now forfeited. Probably the most hard-hitting one was taking me out of kindergarten in one of the best school systems in the country. Instead, I would be in the rural school in Sunrise Beach, Missouri, which did not have a kindergarten class and had a qualitative difference from the Shawnee Mission School District of the 1960s. We were also leaving our friends and moving farther from extended family.

Part of my parents' decision to move to the lake was that

it would be a wonderful place for me to grow up. However, education in a school is an imperative factor in growing up. In early September 1959, I started in kindergarten in the Shawnee Mission School District. The Hurricane Deck Elementary School in Sunrise Beach, Missouri, which is part of the Camdenton School District, did not have kindergarten in 1960. First through third grade students were in one room. The school was a three-room schoolhouse for grades first through eighth. This was a sacrifice my parents were willing to make in 1960. Despite a delay in my education, I learned about many more things at the lake that were not in school. With frogs, toads, lizards, and ducks, it was a rich educational life.

I had a good friend across the street and was sad to move away from him, yet this was a small price to pay. They did come to visit us. Our extended family came to visit us in Kansas City often, but would they come to visit us at the lake? All of these pointed to areas of concern my parents had; however, they did not keep us from moving to the lake. My mom made arrangements with friends and family to move forward. This will be described later in the book.

My father, Bob, was trying to break away from TWA, and he

decided to continue to work for them for at least eighteen more months to provide financial security for our family. During this time, he came home to us at the lake on his days off. By the time he left, he had been with TWA for eighteen years. He had good friends there, and we continued to see them periodically after our total transition to the lake.

These sacrifices helped my mom do things to minimize the impact of the education situation, leaving friends, and the financial security. She took quick action on friends and was flexible with my dad, helping him come and go. She became extremely involved in the school situation and helped to pass the bond election to improve the schools. You will hear more about this in the next chapter.

Chapter 4

MOVING TO THE LAKE: THE ADVENTURE BEGINS

The first two years at the resort seemed like an adventure to me as I reflect back on it and the journey to how we became lake people. We all jumped into lake life with both feet with primarily positive adventures. My father continued to work for TWA, so we continued to have flight benefits. The rest of the adventures were associated with lake life. The stories in this chapter will unfold chronologically.

The first adventure occurred within sixty days of us moving to the lake. During the winter of 1960, after February 1, 1960, the lake received more than sixty inches of snow. My father had arranged for us to be on the first ever nonstop flight by

TWA from New York City to Los Angeles. The only problem was we were snowed in at the resort. My dad's ingenuity and motivation helped us make the trip. We went to Disneyland, and I wanted to find Donald Duck. It was a memorable trip, and it was clear to see why my father was so determined to make it happen.

Shortly after we returned home, we had visitors from the city. My good friend and I had started kindergarten together, and he came down to the lake to see us with his family. We took them to see the Ha Ha Tonka area in Lake South, which was before it became a state park. The winter weather had improved, and we were able to play with the ducks that frequently visited our cove on the lake. We had fun with our friends and had pride in showing them our new home and community.

It was the winter that revealed how our new house was different than anywhere we had lived before. The heat for the house came through a floor furnace. Sleeping with your bedroom door open was required, as the central floor furnace was the only heat in the house. It was fun to stand over the furnace and warm up really quickly.

*Me playing with ducks on the shore during
our first winter at the lake.*

In the spring, my mom cut my hair, and I was enjoying climbing trees while dressed in jeans and a T-shirt. One day my dad arrived, came into the house, and asked my mom, "Who is that little boy outside?"

She laughed and said, "That is your tomboy daughter. She is having fun playing outside." My mom had to help me get down out of the tree I had climbed.

Later in the spring, the lake level came way up, and our resort was flooded. When Truman Lake was created in 1964, these problems stopped. It was alarming to us as new lake people. There was a creek in the back of the cove, and it was full due to so much rain, which was a follow-up from all the winter snow.

The flooded lake in 1960. Our house is the building pictured.

We started seeing our first customers at the resort in the spring of 1960. At this time, many of our customers liked to fish. We sold fishing licenses for both in-state and out-of-state customers, as well as bait, including minnows, worms, and artificial lures. At the resort, we also had boat storage. Most of the nonfishing customers were boat-storage patrons. The boats stored were mainly pleasure boats. My parents both emphasized the importance of providing high-quality service so the customers would have pleasurable experiences. Some of the things that contributed to this included clean cabins with adequate amounts of toilet paper for the duration of their stay, freshly swept sidewalks, responsive service when customers came to the office, and a happy attitude while serving them.

During the month of June 1960, my mother arranged for me to spend about one month with her family in western Kansas who lived on farms and even a dairy farm close to Greensburg and Coldwater, Kanas. This was the beginning of the close relationship with my extended family, including several cousins. One family had a horse, Tipsy, that I loved and was able to ride, which made my heart very happy. I stayed with my grandmother (my mother's mother), at her house. She had showed me the room I would be staying in early in the year, and it had become her storage room for many things she saved.

When I came in the summer, the room was clean and so sunny and pleasant. Noticing all the work she had done for me and others who might stay in this room was quite a confidence booster, as I knew she wanted me there with her. I ended up doing this for one of two more years, and it was fun to spend time with all my cousins, ride Tipsy, and enjoy my family on the farm. One of my best memories of these times was coming home and talking about it with my parents, particularly my dad.

Talking with my dad the night I returned home from Coldwater, Kansas.

As the summer progressed, new things happened. First, my parents found a church that we stayed with for years, Kent Memorial Lutheran (LCA) Church in Sunrise Beach. My parents ensured my participation in Sunday school and vacation Bible school. I also started playing with toads and lizards. These little animals fascinated me. It was fun to scare teenage girls with them, because I could not understand what was scary about the reptiles.

My parents told me I must wear a life belt if I was on the dock, because my parents were not able to closely supervise me, and children can fall into the water and drown. They told me if they caught me on the dock without the life belt, I would be punished by having to stay in the house the entire next day. Oh, of course it happened one time, and they caught me. The day in the house was painful. I never went on the dock without a life belt again. My parents gave me limits to keep me safe.

In August, a group of customers who became regular clientele stayed at the resort. They were all from the same farm town in Kewanee, Illinois. The Petersons usually stayed for two weeks with their two sons, the Newmans with their daughters, and the Novaks with their nephew, Sepi (who was from Czechoslovakia). It was during this week in August that I started waterskiing. It was amazing that I was waterskiing at age five, almost six. This ended up being a fantastic week of summer every year with this group, and we did get to know them well. This was the beginning of skiing for me. The adventures had been extensive and varied during the first few months.

My mom had started having patio parties for the resort customers during this summer, and this provided a great opportunity to get to know them and develop a relationship with them. It usually happened on Sunday evening after they checked in on Saturday.

My mom and I at a patio party.

The Labor Day holiday weekend was big for us, and on the day after the actual holiday, school began at the Hurricane Deck Elementary School. Being in a room with three grades was wild. The third graders seemed so big, and they helped the new first graders (me). My mom joined the PTA and got involved quickly.

Camden County knew they needed to improve schools, and my mom became heavily involved in the bond issue to create the funding for the needed improvements. She got to know two gentlemen who were leading the effort, Jim Risner (owner of the local radio station) and John McCroy (owner of a grocery store). She talked about both of them at home, and I had decided what they looked like, and it ended up that each looked like the other person in my imagination. The bond issue did pass, and the school district immediately started making improvements.

I am the shorter girl, and Ronda is the taller girl.

The other activity I started in first grade was tap dancing lessons. Another girl in my class (Ronda) and I were in lessons together given by her mother, Barbara Bryant. This was fun and enjoyable. We actually had costumes my mom helped make, and we had programs for local community meetings. This helped to fill the quiet winter times as well as other times.

My mom and I played card games, board games, and read. This began my interest in games and reading. Being in a cove, the lake also froze, and I started ice skating on it. With me in school and my mom involved with PTA and the bond issue, the winter flew by.

It was during these years that my interest in animals as playmates began. Early on, I enjoyed reptiles, as the resort had a creek that fed into the lake. I saw tadpoles turn into frogs had fun with them, lizards, and snakes (small red-necked snakes). I played with them for hours on end, and they were good companions to me.

We also had a cat and dog at the resort. Our cat had kittens every year, but we only kept two over the years. One was a yellow tabby I named Sunny. Sunny would let me dress her and play with her as if she was a doll or baby, and she was the only kitten that would allow me to do this. I loved this little cat so much.

The second kitten we kept was a gray tabby named Smoky. She was a nice cat, and my dad was especially fond of her.

Spring arrived, customers started coming, and reservations were coming in for the summer. Once again, my parents emphasized the importance of providing impeccably good service for our customers, with some of the same things they mentioned the year before, such as ensuring each unit had the right amount of toilet paper. We were responsive in answering the office calls, clear about check-in and check-out times, and always had a smile on our faces when doing these things. My job was to ensure the right amount of toilet paper was in each unit when cleaned. This meant calculating the number of people and the number of days the party was staying, so I could do the math to ensure they did not have enough toilet paper to waste but did not have to come get more from the office.

During the summer, several big things occurred. I continued to water-ski and have fun with it. A young couple named Doris and Furl took a significant interest in me. We liked each other very much. They had no children, and we were kindred spirits. I actually went home with them in the city for a few days. We all had fun and liked each other more. They were frequent customers, and our relationship continued to flourish. All summer, I enjoyed being in the water whenever I could. I ended up developing an ear infection that reoccurred many times over the next few years—swimmer's ear.

My mom told the doctor, "I wish we had a swimming pool so this would not happen to her."

The doctor replied, "The lake is actually cleaner that a swimming pool."

Here I am getting ready to jump or dive into the lake on the swimming dock.

In August 1961, the Kewanee group arrived for the second time. We had fun with them and enjoyed them as customers.

The Novaks were Swedish, like my father's father. They actually brought us some things like lingonberries and herring fish. This was the first year we started doing pyramids while we were waterskiing. We had enough people with the Newman girls, the Peterson boys, and me. It was fun to work together with this group to do something spectacular.

Once again, the day after our busy Labor Day holiday weekend, school started. This year, the fall of 1961, I began second grade. There were now two grades in each room. There were sixteen children in my grade, the same kids from last year, and some of them also went to Sunday school with me. It was typical for me not to see school friends in the summer except during Sunday school. We would play in the forest during recess and create rock gardens and other fun structures with rocks. The tap dance lessons continued with Barbara Bryant.

Sometime in the fall, my father left TWA. Soon after, we temporarily moved to Coldwater, Kansas, (where my mother's mother lived) for my dad to do work around the town. My grandmother had helped to set up the work my father did. Coldwater Elementary School was my school for the quarter.

During this time, I became sick with the mumps, which delayed school. Once I began, I was somewhat behind.

Grandma had a get-acquainted party for me with local children. A new friend, Carol Atteberry, became a good friend. She was in my grade, which helped. This time provided the opportunity for me to spend one month with my extended family during the summer coming up once again. We went back to the lake at the end of the quarter with more money and happy to be home. My mother's sister, Ann, came home with us. She helped entertain me and sewed with my mother. She also brought her sheltie dog, Tammie. We had a nice winter playing cards and games, ice skating, tap dancing, attending Sunday school, and playing with the ducks. My mother named one of the ducks Mr. Drake. The quarter we spent in Coldwater made me appreciate my new home at the lake.

Spring began just as it had in the past with customers starting to come in April 1961, and reservations for the summer coming through. Soon after school ended, the trip to Coldwater began. I had a great time with my aunts, uncles, and cousins and enjoyed the wonderful room my grandmother had created just for me. One of my cousins had a horse named Tipsy I had played with since I was three. I enjoyed Tipsy and playing with my cousins. But once home, I was elated to be back at the lake with my parents. I sat on my dad's lap and told him all about my time in the Coldwater area. He was the best listener, and we were happy to be together again.

Here I am with my cousin Pat riding Tipsy in Coldwater, cementing my interest in horses.

The rest of the summer had some of the best and worst times. Shortly after my return, the water well we had at the resort developed some big problems. About this time, my father's father retired from the railroad and moved to the resort with us. He helped my parents with the money to drill a new well. They hit the jackpot, as the new well was an artisanal well, and the water was delicious.

Having my grandfather with us was one of the best parts of the summer. We started fishing and had fun doing this and eating sardines together. He was a wonderful companion for me, and he also started doing work around the resort. We were each doing our respective jobs, with me delivering toilet paper, and Grandfather bringing oil to the dock for boat fuel and sweeping the sidewalks.

The results of fishing with my grandpa. We loved to do this together.

The worst part of the summer was the beginning of my education about the dangers in the lake. Furl and Doris were down for a few days and were having fun on the Grand Glaize arm of the lake close to the bridge. He inadvertently kicked the engine into reverse when he jumped into the water, and the boat backed over, him cutting his leg off. He subsequently died. This was a terrible shock and a horrific accident. I never saw Doris again, and I am sure it destroyed her. Since this terrible accident, a new function in boats was required. A button had to be pushed to put a boat engine in any gear. This tragic event was the beginning of my respect around the lake water.

In August, the Kewanee group arrived again. We continued to have fun waterskiing, playing cards, and swimming. We started as a group, making the trek to Lake Ozark to see the Ozark Opry, a music and comedy show from Lee Mace. My grandfather was able to meet the Petersons and the Novaks, both of whom were Swedish. My grandfather and I continued to be fishing buddies.

After the first two years, the big adventure was about to end. My grandfather brought us some financial stability, as he was paying my parents' rent. He was also a great help at the resort, and we had a nice time together. With this stability, my parents were able to do more planning on how to improve the resort.

In the fall of 1962 when third grade began, my favorite elementary teacher, Mrs. LaVerne Edwards, became my teacher. This year, my mother was also the president of the PTA and was able to get to know Mrs. Edwards well. It was also this fall when my great aunt Lois and uncle Pete (my grandfather's baby brother) started spending their two-week vacation with' us in early October. At Christmas, my mother's sister, Wanda, and her family came to celebrate with us. My father and grandfather started building the open-air recreation room at the resort, as well as the concrete shuffleboard court. It was an exciting winter, and the tap dancing continued.

Chapter 5
DEVELOPING THE RESORT: SETTLING INTO LAKE LIFE

The focus of the next four years was improving the resort and having some fun. 1963–1967 were great years and positioned the resort for a sustainable future. During this time, my father, with my grandfather's assistance, remodeled the stone cabins and built a kiddie pool. My parents also surprised me with an opportunity.

As 1963 began, third grade with Mrs. Edwards was completed. She helped me grow into a stronger reader, so I began reading more. Sunday school at the Lutheran church in Sunrise Beach continued, my dad completed the recreation room, and my parents arranged to have table tennis, pinball machines, and a nickelodeon installed in the space. The nickelodeon was a wonderful addition because we had limited radio at the lake at this time, mainly playing old-time country music. The nickelodeon brought pop music to the resort for all of us.

During the winter, my father decided to take outside carpentry work to supplement our income. Tan-Tar-A Resort was being built at this time, and this is where he was working for a few months in the winter. The winter this year was extremely cold. People were driving cars on the lake, as it was frozen, and even the main channel of the Osage arm of the lake was frozen. My father walked to Tan-Tar-A to work a couple of days. This was so amazing. The lake has not frozen quite like that again. Tan-Tar-A was across the main channel of the lake from our resort. It has always been fun to see Tan-Tar-A evolve, knowing my father was part of building this beautiful high-end resort.

The completed recreation room brought so much fun to the place. We had table tennis, pinball machines, a nickelodeon, and a space to play cards. The nickelodeon gave us popular music for the first time.

The recreation room during construction.

The completed recreation room.

My mother started her rose bushes and canna plants and had very good success with both of these. These created aesthetic beauty at the resort that customers and our family enjoyed. My grandfather helped her with some of the gardening, and both of them adored these activities and their outcomes.

The summer was fun with the recreation room and the equipment in it. This was the first time new music was heard at the resort via the nickelodeon. We had a customer named Larry who was an extremely good table tennis player. He used two crutches to get around, yet he played table tennis like no other. It was fun to see him play. We had a couple of weeks of cooler, rainy weather this summer, and several of us played cards in the recreation room and had fun.

We all swam in the lake and had a fabulous time. Occasionally, someone would spot a snake in the water, and everyone would jump out of the lake. My dad would take a rowboat out or shoot his rifle from the shore and kill the snake. He was everyone's hero. Once again, my parents emphasized the importance of creating impeccable service with each encounter with our customers.

In August, the Kewanee group arrived again this year, and we continued with some of the same things, except Rex Peterson began barefoot waterskiing. It was so exciting. I continued to water-ski and swim throughout the summer and continued to deal with swimmer's ear. This summer, one of my elementary school friends was involved in an accident at the lake where she ran into the prop of a boat engine. She was cut up pretty badly and needed more than one hundred stitches. It was yet another accident at the lake that encouraged respect for the water and the boats in the lake.

In the fall of 1963, I began fourth grade, again with Mrs. Edwards as my teacher. We even had her over to our house for dinner once or twice during the school year. This seemed extremely spectacular. My mom continued to serve as the PTA president. Over the winter, the remodeling of the stone cabins began, which my dad and grandfather were able to complete between the two of them. They also installed the new kiddie pool and patio. It was a busy winter with many projects.

The small pool and shuffleboard area were added entertainment for the guests.

With these new features, my father took new pictures and created a new brochure. We received lists of interested customers from the Lake of the Ozarks Visitors Group, and we joined with two other resorts to send out advertising. We divided the list in thirds, stuffed and addressed the envelopes, and mailed them out. The other resorts we collaborated with were Holly Air and Bass Point. My part was to stuff the envelopes and help seal them. My parents addressed the envelopes and mailed them. This is when we started having hamburgers and malts on Saturday nights. It became a fun tradition.

This fall, I began taking piano lessons and enjoyed it. On Christmas morning, a spinet piano was delivered to our house. I was blown away! I started taking piano lessons more seriously and practicing more. Later in the year was my first piano recital. My grandfather loved to listen to me practice. I did not understand at the time, but as a child, he had loved to listen to his father played the violin in Gothenburg, Sweden. He was my biggest fan.

Winter entertainment and improvement with crappie bed creation and ice fun.

As we moved into 1964, my dad and grandfather remodeled the other two stone cabins. This kept them busy over the winter, and we then had four really nice two-bedroom cabins. The cabins were rented first with reservations and enhanced the resort significantly. Thus, my jobs at the resort expanded. I continued to take toilet paper to the cabins when they were vacant on Saturday and started delivering sheets to cabins to refresh the beds on changeover days. We changed to rent cabins by the week only, from Saturday to Saturday. We also noticed we had a lot of repeat business.

In 1964, the lake was sequestered away from the challenges of the time with the Vietnam War and civil rights demonstrations and events. We were so busy at the lake that we did not really pay much attention, as it did not impact our lives. We watched about things on the news on one of the two television stations we received, and that was our coverage.

In the summer of 1964, we had four newly remodeled stone cabins, a kiddie pool, a nice recreation room, and a shuffleboard court. Business continued much the way it had over the last year as the August Kewanee group arrived again for the usual fun we had as a group, such as the Ozark Opry evening, swimming, and waterskiing.

We all worked around the resort doing our respective jobs.

It was this summer when my dad taught me how to manage the kiddie pool and all that was needed to keep it in good shape. This included managing the chemicals, testing, and vacuuming. The goal was to make it look inviting to our guests. When we completed our work on the pool, we would step back and look at the beauty we created. It was a fabulous reward. The entire mission of our resort was to create a fantastic experience for our guests.

In the summer of 1964, my parents asked me to take over the minnow business at the resort. My job would be to manage the business, take care of all minnow customers, and have a chance to take the profits to save for my goal of purchasing a horse. Of course, I said yes, and this was now my responsibility. I learned how to get fish odor off my hands after getting three dozen minnows so I could continue dinner. I would buy five hundred minnows for $6.75 and then sold them for $1.10 for three dozen. I was not rich, yet I did make profits. I was also able to get customers gas for their boats at the dock. This was fun, as it surprised a lot of the customers, and I made some new lake friends. All of these are lake life responsibilities, and I loved each of them.

In the fall of 1964, I began fifth grade. This was a fun year for me because we would enact a television show called *Hullabaloo* during recess. I was also reading everything I could get my hands on. Sunday school continued, and I received perfect attendance recognition, as my parents ensured I went. At Christmas this year, we took our first vacation to Hot Springs, Arkansas, and New Orleans. We had a nice time and came home renewed and ready to go to work on the resort and back to school. We also took a day trip in the early spring to go look at the Truman Lake Dam, as we had high expectations for what this lake would do to help the Lake of the Ozarks stabilize.

In 1965, we settled into our roles and responsibilities. The resort continued its Saturday-to-Saturday rentals, giving us a busy Saturday every week. My mom started coaching me through the feeling of loss from losing friends each week by reminding me to look forward to the people coming the next week. During this summer, I went to a two-week Girl Scout camp close to Springfield, Missouri. For the first week I was homesick for the resort and the lake, and then I made friends and had fun the second week. When my mom and grandfather picked me up, I was pungent, and they could not ride home with the car windows up. It was wonderful to be home.

Later in the summer in August, the Kewanee group descended on us again with their fun spiritedness and desire to have a great time. Rex continued to barefoot water-ski, and his brother, Kurt, was perfecting his slalom water-ski turns and sprays. We had fun playing the pinball machines and listening to the nickelodeon in the recreation room, as well as waterskiing and swimming.

This was the summer we started going to a restaurant by boat for breakfast. We would go as a group with several boats and convoy to a restaurant by the Grand Glaize Bridge. For us, this was about a five-mile trip—one mile out of our cove and four miles down the lake closer to the Bagnell Dam. This adventure on the water was about thirty minutes of ecstasy. It was so fun to do this as a group! This started a tradition to do this annually with the Kewanee group and expand it to others, and it was added to other traditions, such as our Ozark Opry trek to Lake Ozark.

Chapter 6
ENJOYING OUR LIFE

During the years between 1967 and 1969, we enhanced our resort every year. The features added to the business during the last five years created positive results. We continued to run the business on weekly rentals, and this simplified our lives in the season that ran April through October. My father built an additional three-bedroom cabin with a beautiful deck. He also built a new twenty-by-forty-foot swimming pool next to the kiddie pool. My mother's gardening paid off with beautiful roses and cannas, creating more aesthetic beauty at the resort. In 1967, my goal of getting a horse was reached, and school was enjoyable. We were able to enjoy a vacation during the holiday time of the year and took some very fun trips.

The enhancements created at the resort included the four stone cabins with two bedrooms each; our new three-bedroom cabin with a deck; a brand-new full-size pool and kiddie pool; the recreation room with table tennis, pinball machines, and the amazing nickelodeon for music; as well as top-notch playground equipment and a shuffleboard court. All of these features delighted our customers. We saw this with increased repeat business and reservations being made one full year in advance more often. All of this was built on our basics of being at the back of a beautiful and quiet mile-long cove. We prided ourselves on having stellar customer service and being a full-service resort, including fishing bait and boat fuel, which was all done with a smile and the relationships we had built.

My mother was having extremely good results with her gardening. Over the last few years, she had invested in buying top-quality rose buses, and she planted them in very prominent and sunny locations. There were between six and eight rose bushes by 1969. She tended to them year-round to have them really thrive. Mom tried new colors, such as Tropicana, which combine two colors in each bloom, and she was so proud when the results were perfect. The roses were her first love, yet she also adored the red cannas she coddled. These were in a garden that could be seen from the stone cabins, the pool, and our house. Every fall and spring she would extract the bulbs, put them in a storage container for the winter, and then replant them for their full glory each summer. These were a big part of her year-round life, as well as caring for all of us.

The care she gave all of us was first-rate. She was an excellent cook, ran the reservations for the resort, was involved in the community, helped me in my young life, sewed my clothes, and enjoyed life. She had more time to cook during this time, and we developed the habit of going to the store weekly or biweekly, as the closest grocery store was more than fifteen miles away. Our cabin cleaning helpers from Climax Springs brought fresh tomatoes and corn to us weekly on Saturdays. I can remember drinking home-brewed iced tea at every dinner, having homegrown tomatoes to eat, and tasting all kinds of other things. We also made homemade ice cream occasionally.

Mom had an effective reservation system for the resort and helped us stay very organized. When new people made reservations, she asked if they had children and inquired about their ages. This helped me deal with the high amount of change in the customers at the resort. She would brief me on who was coming the following week, and she let me reflect on the fun of the previous week and look into the coming week with positive expectancy.

Mom did several things to help me. First, she recognized my teeth had problems and got me to an orthodontist to correct the issues. It started at the oral surgeon's office to do some extractions, which resulted in sitting in the dentist chair for nearly three hours one day. The dentist was so worried, yet I completely surprised him with my calm ability to follow instructions. This became about a three-year process with braces and monthly visits to the orthodontist in Springfield, Missouri, which was ninety miles to our southwest.

I remember starting school in seventh and eighth grade with cute corduroy jumpers my mom made and knee socks that matched. We would have fun selecting the patterns and materials for the jumpers. We also found nice shirts and sweaters to wear with the jumpers. This helped me go to school with confidence. My mother also made sure to get me to Sunday school, and in seventh grade, I began a three-year catechism class that continued until ninth grade.

In 1967, the minnow business had made enough money that I was able to save enough to buy a horse. This was one of the best years of my life. On July 2, 1967, a Saturday, my horse was delivered. It was a red-letter day for all of us. I can remember everyone stopped what he or she was doing at the time the horse arrived. This horse was a mare, Koby Lynn, that was half quarter horse and half Welsh pony. She was just the right size for me, as I was petite at this time of my life. She was brown and had a star on her forehead. My father had prepared a place for her with a barn and corral. She had a cantankerous personality. Sometimes, she would be running up the gravel road and quickly turn right, and I would fall off. She would run off, and we would have to chase her, catch her, and ride her home. We even hobbled her sometimes to keep her home, yet she learned to run that way. My parents helped with her in many ways to manage her care. We needed to board her in the winter, and my father would set that up and help me take care of her. My father and I took many trips to get hay for food. We would load it and then unload it at home. I think he was surprised at how hard I worked for my horse. We had Koby Lynn for two years and eventually traded her in for a bigger horse.

My new horse was a gelding, and his name was Chief. He was a long-legged, dappled Appaloosa and was majestic looking. He was the perfect horse, and we had him three years. Fun with Chief was normal. I could ride him bareback or lie next to his neck, and he could take me up the forested hill without touching a branch on me. He was a wonderful partner when my grandfather and I would go blackberry picking. He would help us carry the goods down the hill. Chief would stay around and graze on the lawn, and he was trustworthy. I never fell off of him.

Chief was a fun horse to ride, and we were a great team.

In 1967, I began seventh grade at Hurricane Deck Elementary School. Our teacher was the school principal, Mr. Charles DeJarnete. By this time, I had read a lot, primarily the Hardy Boys, Nancy Drew, and Bobbsey Twins series. In this grade, I felt mentally challenged and capable like never before. Seventh grade was my favorite year in school.

In September, I was able to get up on one water ski. I had worked on this for one year, and finally, on one September day after school when my parents took me skiing, I did it. It was a wonderful accomplishment, and I was proud of myself. I was extremely petite, and this created challenges, yet my arms were strong enough to get me out of the water at age twelve. Overall, this year was one of the best years of my life with the horse accomplishment, skiing on one water ski, and seventh-grade success.

This was the year we continued vacationing during the winter holiday. This was the off season at the resort, and I was out of school for two weeks. We started going to Florida. To get ready, my mom and I made Christmas tree decorations that could travel. We packed our portable tree and decorations, and off we went to the Sunshine State. We drove the long way by going first to Savannah, Georgia, and then into Florida. We made it to Daytona Beach, Florida, and stayed at the Hawaiian Inn. We put up our tree, decorated it, and had a fabulous Christmas. I actually made a friend with a girl my age in the room next door. Her name was Debbie, and home for her was Homer, New York. We became fast friends, continued to be pen pals, and saw each other two more times at the Hawaiian Inn in Daytona Beach.

In 1968 and 1969, our business continued to grow with reservations and repeat business. We started seeing many customers for reoccurring summer vacations. It was fun for me because I met friends in the summer, wrote to them in the winter, and saw them again the next summer. Also, during these years, my parents opened up part of the vacant property in the forty acres that made up the resort into an area for large mobile homes. Several of our best repeat customers took advantage of this opportunity.

The first customers were the Petersons from Kewanee. They had demonstrated a strong interest in the lake, and this proved to be true. Then they became a boat storage customer. The two boys, Rex and Kurt, started coming down by themselves at times. Another repeat customer, the Petersons from Florissant, Missouri, (a suburb of St. Louis), also became a mobile home customer. Both of these customers were favorites of mine because I had so much fun with the children. The St. Louis Petersons had a daughter about my age. We enjoyed each other's company, and I went home with them to Florissant a couple of times. This lake girl in the city was the opportunity for me.

Chapter 7
THE LAST THREE YEARS IN THE RESORT

During the fall of 1968, I became good friends with a new friend in the consolidated middle school who also loved horses. Her name was Janice. We talked about horses, schoolwork, and other important issues to fourteen-year-old girls. She invited me into a Masonic organization for young women called the Rainbow Girls. I stayed involved with this group throughout my high school years and eventually became the leader of our chapter. It was fun, as it gave me the opportunity to develop and show my leadership skills and occasionally get dressed up in formal wear.

In late 1968, we vacationed in Florida again during the

holiday break. It was fun because we knew more about what we wanted to do. We met the friends from Homer, New York, at the Hawaiian Inn in Daytona Beach for Christmas again and had even more fun with them than the year before. We left Daytona Beach and headed south to Miami and into the Florida Keys. It was a wonderful trip and gave us a big break from the resort, school, and cold weather.

1969 began with us coming home from our vacation and getting focused for the new year ahead. We already had many reservations for the summer. Our newly remodeled cabins and the new cabin were popular, and the pool was a valuable addition. Our new brochure showcased all of the updates. We continued to cooperate with other resorts for marketing, which required the stuffing, addressing, and mailing of envelopes.

I was now going to school in Camdenton for middle school, and this was the first time middle school was offered. It was a consolidated school with elementary schools from Sunrise Beach, Osage Beach, and Climax Springs all combined together at the school. Camdenton was about seventeen miles from the resort. My mother negotiated with the bus company that they would pick me up at my house, coming down the one-mile gravel road to get me. This was the first year for this kind of bus service.

The summer of 1969 was a fun year for us at the resort. We continued to enjoy about 45 percent repeat business, and reservations were made early, providing the promise of another successful summer. Our weeklong rentals continued to be of high value to us as resort owners. It gave us one super busy day per week—Saturday. We had help from the same people to clean the cabins, while my father and I made the beds, and my grandfather and mother did everything else with customers checking in and leaving. We also had Chief to attend to and ensure he was a happy horse.

This was a fun summer for me at fifteen years old. I was able to do more, such as help my father make beds on Saturday, and sometimes I would do this myself if he were pulled away to launch a boat or do something else important. I was able to read well, and this was the summer I started reading adult books. The first book I read was *Valley of the Dolls*, which really opened my eyes to other kinds of lives. It also fueled my desire to read.

I had more skills to meet new people and make friends fast. This was also the summer my father bought a small hydroplane.

It had a little outboard motor on it. My parents told me I could take it out so long as I had on a life jacket and remained in the cove. I was not to go out into the main channel with it. I was sure they meant business and honored their wishes. It was a lot of fun, and boating by myself was enjoyable at times.

This was the first summer when an interest in boys surfaced. One boy, who was the son of a repeat customer, was Craig Mendenhall from a suburb of Kansas City. He was funny, and we both loved to water-ski. We were so proud when we both decided to get matching slalom skis and life jackets. We even tried to come out of the water together on our new skis and had fun. I had also made a friend with a girl in my elementary class, Vicki, and we saw each other during the summer at both of our homes. When we were at her house, it was a quiet, private cove, and we went skinny-dipping in the lake. It was fun, and we giggled so much.

The August Kewanee group continued to visit, and it became better because the Petersons were now mobile-home owners. We continued to do our group boat breakfast to the Grand Glaize area for more fun. All of us kids were getting older, so we enjoyed the recreation room with the pinball machines and listened to music with the nickelodeon.

During this time, my cousins, Toni and Paulette, both came to stay with us for two weeks. Because we were all about the same age, we had fun. This included swimming, skiing, playing cards and games, listening to music, talking, playing with Chief, and playing pinball. I have a picture with Paulette and me standing with Chief as he was having his horseshoes changed. My father and I continued to have fun getting hay, which was an important activity.

This summer, I also started working in an old-fashioned soda fountain. The work was enjoyable because the soda fountain was a big success. I was working on the July night when the astronauts landed on the moon. One of my coworkers and I had fun with a customer as we got tickled and laughed, and he commented how he wished he could be so happy without substances. Our rule was we could have only one milkshake a day. It was fun to make old-fashioned phosphate sodas, ice cream sodas, ice cream sundaes, and banana splits. Many evenings over the summer, customers were lined up outside the building to have ice cream. This put the pressure on us to work hard.

In the fall of 1969, my father wanted us to move out of our house so he could completely remodel it. My grandfather stayed in his room in a different part of the house. We moved into stone cabin one for the winter. We made this move in early October.

My parents also decided to buy a new boat for a rental boat at the resort. They picked it up in Waukegan, Illinois, just north of Chicago. Right after they left that morning, the phone rang as I was getting ready to leave for school. It was Craig Mendenhall's aunt calling to tell us he had died the night before in a car accident. I conveyed my deepest condolences and was shocked and saddened. It was a huge loss; he was just sixteen. I could not contact my parents, and I had to keep going and get on the school bus for the day.

I was now a sophomore in high school. School started out with a team project to decorate a hallway in the school for homecoming. Our theme was space with foil-lined walls. The only problem was it needed to be fastened every day, as aluminum foil is heavy. We, as a group, had fun doing this with each day's retape. I don't remember if we won the prize or not; the prize was the fun we had.

This was the school year I made more friends. On my fifteenth birthday in October, I had a slumber party with a few friends. On my birthday night, my monthly period started. I was aghast. It was clear what was happening, yet I was so embarrassed on this particular day. As I reflect on it, there is no doubt I started my period on my fifteenth birthday—an easy date to remember.

During this school year, I continued my involvement with Rainbow Girls and then started getting involved in the youth group at church. It included many of the children I went to Hurricane Deck School with, yet it included several grades. We had a lot of fun and did the church service occasionally. I had the opportunity to deliver the message at one of these and talked about the power of love. It was exciting, challenging, and fun. It was my first public speaking experience, and I loved it.

My father was busy with the house remodel, and my grandfather helped. The winter flew by, but with this project being so important, we did not do a vacation during the holidays this year. We had a fun Christmas in cabin one and put all our energy into completing the project. The newly remodeled house would be worth the work. This project gutted the house, put a new roof on it, and added some square footage. My mom wanted a nice kitchen, a patio, and a master bedroom. I wanted a bigger bedroom and a better HVAC system for the house. They had a deadline in time to rent cabin one for the next season: May 1, 1970. My dad hired some workers to help.

We were thrilled with the house when it was complete in the spring of 1970. We all had just what we wanted. The HVAC system now included heat and air conditioning throughout the house. We all loved the patio, which had a view of the pools, flowers, lake, and resort. We were able to get cabin one ready for renting just in time, and we were overjoyed to be in our newly refurbished house. We continued to get the resort ready for the 1970 season.

My sophomore year in high school was now complete. Some of my courses included biology, geometry, world history, English, and band. I was playing the clarinet. I was a first clarinet, yet I could not get to be first chair, as one of my fellow clarinet-playing colleagues was always better than me. His name was Lynn Zimmer, and he ended up playing the clarinet professionally. Both of those were my loves at this time, as well as the piano, the horse, and waterskiing. The summer ahead looked good with 40 percent repeat business, and nearly 60 percent of the summer was already fully booked with reservations.

The summer of 1970 was a regular summer for me. Our Saturdays seemed to stay busy, and the other days each week were incidental things. Some of our repeat customers were becoming important to me. The Robertses had four children, including twin girls who were my age. They introduced me to drinking alcohol in their cabin. We had a lot of fun together swimming and waterskiing.

A boy was of interest to me this summer in July. His name was Donny. He was about four years older than me and was both nice and good-looking. One day he got tied up in a ski rope, and it left burns and cuts on his arm that looked terrible. He went home, and we did not stay in touch. I continued to work at the soda fountain and with more hours.

My cousin Paulette from Coldwater, Kansas, came to visit for two weeks in August, close to the week the Kewanee group arrived. She was not feeling too well toward the end of our time together, so my mom took her to the doctor. We went on and enjoyed our time together. We continued with the boat caravan to breakfast, Ozark Opry, waterskiing, swimming, and recreation room entertainment. I continued to love to ride and attend to Chief.

When school started in September 1970, I was a junior in high school. Shortly after school began, a boy a year older than me asked me out. We were in band together and primarily got to know each other that way. His name was John Deubler, and he lived in Camdenton. He told me his dad would give him a rough time about taking me out because to take me to a movie in Lake Ozark, he would have to drive the thirty-four-mile round trip to pick me up and drive to Lake Ozark and then repeat the thirty-four-mile round trip to bring me home. My mom told me to remind him that he knew where I lived, and if he wanted to take me to the movie, that was his choice. That stopped all of this. He bought me roses for my sixteenth birthday. We would see each other at school, at band engagements for football games and band contests, and dates.

In mid-September, Paulette called and wanted me to be in her wedding. She was marrying Ron, who was five years older than her. I made a decision I have lived to regret. I chose to go to homecoming and not be in her wedding. She ended up being married to him for twenty-three years and had three children.

Also, one of my best girlfriends, Kathy, had a brother who was two years younger. Being friends with him and his friends was fun. John and I had a lot of fun until about March, and then we broke up. He started dating another person, and I found it painful to see him with her at school. The junior class prepared for prom. We were doing it at the Lake Valley Country Club with the theme of a Japanese garden. We enjoyed preparing. I had a date with a boy who went to school in Versailles, Missouri, so he came to my prom, and I went to the Versailles prom with him. Kathy also had a date from Versailles, so we double-dated for both proms. It turned out pretty well and was a pleasant surprise.

We were enjoying our new house at the beginning of the summer. The resort was operating much as it did last summer with repeat business and advance reservations. Our Saturdays stayed busy, and the rest of the week was quieter. Chief was doing great and was fun to have in our family, yet my grandfather was taking care of him more than I was. It was time to think about going to college and what this meant for Chief. We made a decision to sell him, and it was sad because I did not say goodbye to him. I have lived to regret this greatly.

I was now making beds on Saturday with my dad when he was available. I continued to do the minnow business with the goal of feeding my horse. John reached out to me in mid-June and wanted to take me out and talk about getting back together. We set the date for mid-July to go see the movie *Love Story* and have a nice dinner beforehand at Arrowhead Restaurant in Lake Ozark. He had graduated from high school and was accepted to go to college at Central Missouri State University in Warrensburg, Missouri, which was about ninety miles north and west of the lake on the way to Kansas City. He was working at a grocery store during this summer and only had Saturday off. We agreed to spend Saturday together at the resort. He helped me make beds, and I paid him half of what I made ($4). Once we completed our work, we had the pool to ourselves, as new customers had not checked in yet at that time of day. We spent busy Saturday mornings working hard in the morning with the afternoon as pure relaxation at the pool. This was a fun summer with Saturdays as something to look forward to for me. I continued to work at the soda fountain and took Saturday nights off. Both of the Peterson families were at the resort more with their mobile homes, and we continued to have many other repeat customers such as the Mendenhals. It was so sad to see what had happened to Craig's father after his death. He had been a fun and humorous man who lost all of that.

When the Kewanee group arrived, we continued with our boat to breakfast and Ozark Opry caravans, as well as the fun around the resort. The soda fountain associates gave me a congratulations party to send me off to college. The resort was looking top-notch, and our units were virtually brand new.

Now we had a twenty-by-forty-foot pool with a slide, and our resort looked in tip-top shape.

During the early spring of my senior year, we sponsored a pool party at the resort with teenagers from two clubs I was involved with at my school: Modern Music Masters and Science Club. As the president of both groups, the party was a wonderful way to celebrate the year. The kids who participated in the pool party were amazed at the fun we had and loved the resort. They said it was a fun and enlightening event for them. I was proud of where I lived at the resort.

Central Missouri State University was my college of choice, and I would be attending one year behind John. He picked me up to go to college in his pretty blue Chevy Malibu on a lovely sunny day in early September. The fact that Warrensburg was about ninety miles from home made me happy. My early decision for a major was in science, and I decided to work toward a degree in medical technology. My first few classes included biology, history, English, and lifesaving. At the first lifesaving class, I partnered with a student named Gail, who ended up recruiting me into her sorority, Delta Zeta, and became my pledge mom. Shortly after this, I broke up with John. It was the best thing at the time.

The first time my parents came to visit me was about three

weeks into the school year. We were sitting in the student union café when they told me, "We sold the resort. I was calling the realtor to take it off the market, she was calling me to tell me she had a possible buyer, and we both got a busy signal. She came ahead to see the resort, and they offered the asking price."

I was shocked! My initial reaction was bittersweet. First, I was sad because of what we were moving from, as this had been our life for thirteen years. Yet, at eighteen, I could now do other things with my life. I wondered what those things might be. My parents went on to tell me that the buyers wanted possession and closing to be close to the new year, mid-January 1973. Wow! This was going to be a time of mega transition for all of us.

Chapter 8
TRANSITION OUT OF THE RESORT AND LAKE GIRL QUALITIES

Once my parents left me at college, they put the pedal to the metal to determine their next steps. College courses and sorority rush kept me busy, and it was surprising how fast the time moved. Within the month, they told me they found a nice amount of lakefront property they wanted to buy. It was a multiacre property that had a point and covered a cove area off of Lake Road 5-58 on the 41 mile marker of the Osage Channel. They decided to build a house on the point and knew it would not be ready to move into for about a year, so they temporarily moved to a rental house in Camelot Estates subdivision on Highway 5, north of Camdenton. They had told all the mobile home customers and many of the other frequent repeat customers that they had sold the resort. During that holiday break, we went to south Texas for a short two weeks.

By the time I came home to see my parents in early 1973, they were in the rental house in Camelot Estates. They had decided to get into real estate at the lake and were working on getting their respective real estate licenses. My grandfather was now retired at age seventy-seven. I was excited they decided to stay at the lake. They found a small office in the Greenview area for their real estate business. My father quickly earned his real estate broker license, and my mother eventually passed her real estate license after three tries. They now had their future direction at age fifty and were ready to move forward into real estate. They subsequently helped several people get into the real estate business.

I was busy with my college courses and sorority. Early on, I discovered science was not my cup of tea when I had to look at plants through a microscope in my botany class. I had also taken chemistry. I needed to come up with a new direction for myself.

In the summer of 1973, I was the lifeguard at the Camelot Estates community swimming pool. I was making $2.50 an hour and felt on top of the world. I was at the pool several hours a day and mainly enforcing rules such as no running or diving. One day, a man with extremely long hair entered the pool. At first, I was scared, but I made myself talk with him. His name was Bruce, and he was nice. He drove a hot car—a 1965 GTO. It was beneficial to give him a chance. He was quite a gentleman. By the time the summer went by, I had some ideas about my future.

The Delta Zeta women were having their summer meeting in Lake Ozark, and I went for the Saturday night meeting. We had tickets to ride on the *Larry Don*, a large yacht that had live bands and dancing and cruised the lake from ten until midnight. We were waiting in the parking lot drinking beer, and the Lake Ozark police arrested eight of us for underage drinking. Well, we missed the *Larry Don*, and we each needed $50. I took a chance and called my parents, and yes, they could help and had to drive fifty miles one way to help. I told each woman my parents' address, and they had to pay them back. One hour later, my parents arrived to bail us all out. My father told me months later everyone paid them back except for one person. Sad! It made us take more care of drinking underage.

The house on the point was taking shape by the time I went back to college in the fall of 1973. I talked with an academic counselor and decided to change my major to vocational home economics. This major required all the sciences I had already taken, such as biology, botany, and chemistry I and II, so nothing was lost. Yay! Nutrition and genetics were two of my favorite classes, and science was a prerequisite for both of those courses.

The sorority was going well, and this was a large part of my education in college as an only child. Six of us shared a bathroom in a way that enabled us to keep relationships working. The main fundraiser for the Delta Zeta organization at this time was creating personal flower corsages for the homecoming event. We worked together as a group to make all of this happen and then had the opportunity to see the results of our work with the people wearing them all over campus. It was a fantastic team builder for us as a group of women.

I dated a number of different men during college, so I always had a date for our annual sorority formal dance event.

In the spring of 1974, I brought two sorority sisters to the lake for the weekend. Debbie, Sally, and I worked very hard on a Friday afternoon in May to get the boat ready to launch and use. The next morning, my father took us and the boat to a launch location close to the new house. I started the boat and headed out of the cove, and it started going in a circle. I turned it off, and we paddled it back to the launch location. My father worked hard to get the boat back on the trailer. Then when we tried to pull out, the truck was stuck in the mud. It was a morning when everything that could go wrong did. He said he had never been so happy to pay for boat insurance.

I ended up ruining the lower unit on the inboard/outboard boat. My father had been so kind and calm, and we laughed about it. Both Debbie and Sally were blown away by my dad's calm. The boat was out of commission until early August. It was a costly problem in many ways.

In the early spring of 1974, my parents had moved from the rental house in Camelot Estates to the house they were building. It was mostly done and livable. It was a beautiful house on a point on the 41mile marker of the lake. My parents had taken the boat with them, so a dock was installed in the cove side of the point. My parents hired Kurt Peterson for the summer to help lay railroad ties to tier the landscape to the house. He was on a break from veterinary school at the University of Illinois.

One weekend day in August, we took the boat out for some fun. We had to swim it back to the dock, but it ended up being an easy fix. It was a memorable day for both of us.

That summer I worked in the back office of a local bank. It was fascinating to see the operations at that time. One of the women I worked with had lost her husband to drowning. He had gone fishing one day and never came home. His boat was found, but he was not. More than six months later, his body was recovered from the lake. It was yet another lesson in respect for the lake water. My heart went out to her.

Shortly after the summer ended, three of our repeat customers decided to build houses in the cove my parents were developing. This included the Kewanee Petersons, the Mendenhals, and the Roberts My parents were ecstatic. All of these people had become their friends. Eventually, the entire cove was built out. My parents and grandfather ended up living in this house from 1974 to 1992.

In the mid-1970s, my mother decided one day she hated

living on a gravel road, and this motivated her to check with the county about how to get the road asphalted. The county told her the residents needed to pay 50 percent of the cost, and then it would be scheduled. My mother was then motivated to start contacting all the residents on Lake Road 5-58. She had great results, and the road was asphalted. This demonstrates her ability set a goal, work hard, and make things happen.

When I went back to college in the fall of 1974, I was more involved in the courses in my major. They were enjoyable, and I also had fun with the sorority women. One specifically, Debbie, became one of my best friends. We were roommates, and I helped her be elected as sorority president. Our mum sale was successful again this year, and we had a good pledge class.

My family did vacation in Florida again during this holiday period. We focused on Disney World, as it was now open. We also went to Miami and enjoyed some scenic spots in the city such as Viscaya. We enjoyed the time together, and we came back in time for me to head back to college.

In early 1975, I was deep in my major and finding the courses valuable and interesting. As a junior, the methods of teaching and similar material were the courses. I also took a tailoring course and hand tailored a new coat for myself in the class. I knew I had two general studies courses I still needed to take, including American masterpieces and a sociology class—both with massive amounts of reading. I chose to put these on my schedule for summer school.

As a lake girl, it was apparent that massive amounts of reading at the pool could be possible. Two of my sorority sisters also wanted to do summer school, so we decided to find summer housing for us as a group. Doing these courses would allow me to graduate in May 1976. I did attend summer school, read a lot at the pool, and used CliffsNotes. I worked hard on both the literature and sociology course. I also had some fun with my college colleagues in summer school. I came home at the end of the summer term and slept. My mother woke me up at two o'clock one afternoon to let me know I had a B in American masterpieces. I was so elated. I enjoyed the break at home for three weeks to rest before my senior year.

My parents were getting deeper into the real estate business. It was one of the years my mother was the Lake of the Ozarks Realtor of the Year. They were really having the time of their lives. My grandfather treated them to trips to

Hawaii and Florida. He enjoyed going also and appreciated their companionship.

My grandfather looking sharp on vacation.

I was heavily involved in coursework to prepare me to be a teacher in a high school. I was not sure I wanted to be a teacher, yet I enjoyed the coursework. Two obstacles remained to graduate: living in the home management house for one month and completing student teaching for about ten weeks. Once I did both, I thought I could be a teacher if needed.

By then, I had been accepted into a rehabilitation

counseling master's program at the University of Nebraska and had a fellowship. This was an interest because of my aunt Ann, who was disabled. I also worked as a support person to a blind student while in college and enjoyed it. Once I graduated, that was my direction. After graduation, I went back to the lake for the summer and did waitress work in a nice restaurant for the summer. My mother and I went to Lincoln, Nebraska, to find a place for me to live in July. Both of my parents came with me for the final drop-off in late August. It was the first time I had seen tears in my father's eyes at the parting. I completely understood. Now, I was seven hours from the lake and them.

I began the program at UNL and found it to be excellent. I loved the coursework and was very happy with my decision to do this instead of teaching. Courses included counseling theories, vocational theories, and human development. I was dismayed no one in Nebraska had really heard of the Lake of the Ozarks and bragged about lakes in Nebraska.

I did an internship at the Rehabilitation Institute of Kansas City in the summer of 1977. They had a combination of medical rehabilitation and vocational training. It was wonderful to be closer to home during the summer. This provided a great opportunity to understand both aspects of rehabilitation counseling. In the fall of 1977, I went back to Lincoln to complete my coursework in the master's program, and I graduated in December 1977. I quickly accepted a position as a manager of vocational counseling and independent living at the Nebraska Center for Women in York, Nebraska. I did go home for the holidays after graduating and before my new position started in January 1978. I was homesick for the lake and my family.

When I came home, my family was having a fabulous time in real estate. More of the cove property had been bought, and my dad was considering building rental houses at the top of the hill where there were killer views of the lake. We took a quick trip to southern Texas for the holidays before I went back to Nebraska. It was fun!

We had all transitioned from the resort very well. I had my career direction going, my parents did too, and my grandfather was retired and reading many magazines and newspapers, staying current on what was going on in the world.

I have taken much from what I have learned about the lake,

values, and the ability to live in the now. The lake is a huge body of water. It can be dangerous and must be respected. I have seen several tragic things as a result of carelessness around the water, and I have overly instilled this with my children. We do not go out at night on the water. Kids must wear life jackets until they pass intermediate swim lessons. And there is to be no drinking and driving!

Chapter 9
LAKE GIRL FOR LIFE

I have traveled to many places personally and professionally. I have never found a place quite like the Lake of the Ozarks. It is a large, privately owned lake and has a power-generating dam that minimizes using fossil fuels for power. I have chosen the lake as a place I love to spend time. It is fun and beautiful.

My values are to do what you love, have fun doing what you love, live a positive and affirmative life focused on possibility, be kind, treat others with respect, understand your customer, and try to delight them. I have also frequently told my children that I love them and wanted them. You can do anything with the help and support of your family.

Living in the now can be challenging. I learned to live in

the now at the resort all the time. Each season had it goodness. Each day of each week had goodness in it, and making the most of that time is valuable. That is why the present is the present.

In 1979, I met the man I thought might be my life partner. I was clear with him from the beginning regarding my background and my goals. I was still living in Nebraska and wanted to move to Kansas City to be closer to the lake. He was looking at an honorable discharge from the US Navy in November after a six-year enlistment. When he came to visit me in August for ten days, I had to get him to the lake. He had relevant experience only in the ocean in the northeastern United States and in southern Florida.

My parents had the house on the point until 1992. Our son, Erik, was born in 1984 and daughter, Kerstin, in 1993. Both were introduced to water as young babies, as I knew they would always be around water. We spend much of our free time and holiday time at the lake with my parents. When my mother became bedridden and subsequently died, my father sold the house on the point and bought a house on the 13 mile marker.

Erik spent time with my father at the lake when he was about seven. They had fun, and my father taught him how to fish, mow, and do other things around the house. My father decided he wanted to move back to the city because he was tired of quiet at the lake. My mom died in 1993 and my grandfather in 1994. My father was now free to do exactly as he pleased. When we would go to his house without him, it was so strange. He decided to sell this house in 2002.

We now had a boat with no trailer and no place to stay. I checked with several resorts I knew about from advertising at the resort, and no one would take us for a weekend. I finally called Shangri-La. Yes, they would take us, which surprised me. I guess they have abandoned the weekly rental position. We stayed one weekend in one of the stone cabins. As soon as I opened the sliding door into the unit, the smell overwhelmed me. It was the same smell they had before my father remodeled them. Then I realized that these cabins were older now remodeled than they were when my father remodeled them in 1964. Wow! As I looked around, I realized turquoise refrigerators are not available today. The cabins had not been updated since my parents sold the resort in 1973. Holy cow! I also found many lizards like I had loved to play with as a kid. It was a wild weekend.

On the Monday of that weekend, we took a boat ride down to the 41 mile marker. We found a condo complex that was brand new that really piqued our interest. When we came home, I told my father about it. About two weeks later, my father and I were having lunch out, and he told me he would like to take the proceeds from the sale of two properties to use as the down payment on the condo we found. I wanted to run through the restaurant screaming in elation.

We closed on the condo and moved in on November 2, 2002. It was wonderful to have a presence at the lake. We made friends at the condo, I took two-week vacations when I was working, and we spent a lot of time there when I was between positions. I started doing things with it like hosting a group of work associates for the weekend, and that went on for fifteen years. In the summer of 2017, we transitioned to a lake house. We are now lake house owners, and I love to spend time at the lake. I have secured weekends to spend with each child and their families so we can have fun together. I also want them to hear about respecting the water for safety over and over. The presence at the lake is important to me, and my children seem to love it too. They are also involved two weekends a year to help do work around the house. The goal is to have fun doing work around the house.

The life I had at the resort and lake as a child has impacted me significantly. First, growing up with two positive parents made me positive also. I am very much a goal-driven person, deciding what I want and working to achieve it. The change of all customers weekly has made me open to change, yet I want to know the positive expectation to come from the change. I am open to risk and change and often feel like the scene in Indiana Jones, as if I am stepping off the cliff to find a ledge to stand on. I have also developed skills to live in the present moment and not live with negativity. All of the experiences with my parents and the resort have created a strong work ethic in me. I love what my young life created and how it transitioned within me to my adulthood.

Chapter 10

LAKE CHALLENGES

I have lived or been around the Lake of the Ozarks for sixty years. I love the lake and have seen things that many others would say make the lake challenging. They focus on boats, traffic, highway infrastructure, and the shoreline. Since the lake is privately owned, it has some challenges that public lakes may not have.

The first challenge is the size of boats on the lake. Large cabin cruisers are a problem because of the big wakes they generate. Large pleasure boats and speedboats also put off large waves. This makes it tough for smaller boats such as a seventeen-foot ski boat. I will not go out on the water on the weekends closer to the dam. This was even true when my father had a house on the 13 mile marker in the late 1990s. There is not a governing body to determine the appropriate size boat for this lake, and there is not a way to enforce this size limitation.

Highway infrastructure is improving around the lake. It seems the lake gets ignored from the state because it is a privately owned lake. It does not take long to see this if you take Highway MM to Highway TT when a car comes across the Community Toll Bridge. The Community Bridge had to be privately built. Highway 5 needs attention farther north past the Niangua Bridge. The improvements for Highway 54 have made moving through Osage Beach and Lake Ozark much easier. Attention is needed on the other highways. I think it is sad that a lot of destruction happens to buildings around the lake.

Many of these buildings hold historical significance, and then they are gone.

The shoreline seems to be filling up. The one-mile-long cove the resort is in is now full of docks and buildings looking both good and poor. Other coves are also filling up. I don't know if Ameren, Missouri, has any governance on this.

The immediate challenge and the biggest issue facing the Lake of the Ozarks are the sizes of boats. The lake has a reputation for being rough in the boat-testing world. Also, the entire lake is not like this, and this is not publicized.

I thought when I became an orphan (both of my parents are now deceased and are buried just south of Camdenton) that I would be wanting to fly. The opposite happened to me. I had a desire to go deeper into my roots, and this surprised me. The lake is part of this and is a large portion of my roots.

I love the lake and the experiences I have when I am there. I have pride in the communities around the lake and love both the quiet side of the lake for living and the cosmopolitan side for other things such as shopping and dining. It is exciting to me when both of my children want to go to the lake and introduce their children, my grandchildren, to the lake and all it has to offer. I think the lake is magical, as I have experienced this magic, and I have friends who have also experienced the magic of the water. It is a wonderful place to vacation, relax, and live.

Appendix 1

FACTS ABOUT THE LAKE OF THE OZARKS

The water facts of the lake are worth mentioning. There are several rivers that feed into the main part of the lake, which is the Osage River. The Niangua River meanders into the lake through both the Big and Little Niangua rivers. This primarily goes from the Lake South area to the Lake West area. The Grand Glaize River comes into the lake within the Lake of the Ozarks State Park in the Lake East area. The Gravois River enters the Lake in Lake West in Gravois Mills.

All of these rivers are flowing into the Osage River, which is commonly called the Main Channel of the Lake, and this creates a lake with flow in and out. When Truman Lake was created in 1964, it helped the Lake of the Ozarks tremendously. Truman Lake is a US Army Corp of Engineers lake, and the two lakes meet close to Warsaw, Missouri. The full reservoir of the lake is at 660 feet elevation. Since Truman Lake has been installed, the lake has stabilized and does not go beyond this level. Before Truman Lake was created, flooding was a common occurrence, and this created other issues with driftwood and other things in the water making boating a challenge.

The additional impact Truman Lake has had on the Lake of the Ozarks is the quickness of the water clarity. Before Truman, the lake would be murky until August 1. Now it clears up sooner and may be clear in early or mid-June, so swimming in the water is a more pleasurable experience earlier in the summer.

The shimmering lake is the central part of a vibrant region that consists of more than a dozen communities. The surrounding territory has far-reaching forests, rolling hills, and dramatic bluffs that provide the backdrop to the lake's 1,150-plus miles of meandering shoreline. In summary, this is a privately owned lake that is almost one hundred miles long and has more shoreline than California. This has huge implications for those who call this area home.

The main communities of the lake are the Lake East, Lake North, Lake South, and Lake West. Lake East is on the east side of the lake where you will find the city of Osage Beach and Lake of the Ozarks State Park. You will find excellent shopping along Highway 54, which includes an outlet mall with more than 110 stores, including antique shops, import stores, art galleries, and other specialty boutiques. There are also fun things such as go-karts, mini golf, arcades, parasailing, an indoor water park, evening entertainment, and family fun centers. There are also beautiful resorts and fabulous dining opportunities. Lake of the Ozarks State Park is also in Lake East. It is a large park that offers public beaches, camping, hiking, bicycle trails, horseback riding, marinas, and boat launches. When you drive through it by boat, it has many miles of undisturbed shoreline and tranquility.

Lake North is where the lake began with Bagnell Dam. The construction of this dam was supervised and managed by Union Electric, now Ameren, Missouri, at the Willmore Lodge, a 6,500-square-foot, 1930s, Adirondack-style lodge. Today, it is listed on the National Register of Historic Places and houses the Lake of the Ozarks Chamber of Commerce and a fascinating museum about the Osage River, as well as the incredible construction project that became Bagnell Dam and the Lake of the Ozarks.

Along with Willmore Lodge, Lake North has several communities of Lake Ozark, Bagnell, Eldon, Four Seasons, and Rocky Mount. The historic Bagnell Dam strip has delighted many generations of families with nostalgic appeal, shopping, arcades, and diverse attractions. Lodging within this part of the lake includes numerous mom-and-pop waterfront resorts, bed-and-breakfasts, cabins, condos, hotels, motels, and luxury resorts.

Lake South includes Camdenton (the Camden County Seat), Linn Creek (the historic town destroyed when the Lake was filled in 1931), and Macks Creek, along with Ha Ha Tonka State Park. Ha Ha Tonka features the bluff top ruins of an early twentieth-century castle that was destroyed by fire. Ha Ha Tonka also has fascinating karst topography of caves, sinkholes, glades, savannas, and a powerful spring. The park is accessible by car or boat. Lake South has museums in the new downtown Linn Creek and an annual Dogwood Festival to showcase the Ozark hills when they bloom with pristine, white flowering trees in the spring. Bridal Cave is also in Lake South, where more than two thousand weddings have been performed among the giant columns, delicate soda straws, giant draperies, and Mystery Lake. The cave is accessible by car or boat at the 10.5 mile marker of the Big Niangua arm. Golf courses, great shopping, superb wineries, and other delights are available at the south side of the lake.

Lake West is known as the quiet side of the lake. This is changing, however, since a privately built community bridge was completed in 1998. It connects Highway 5 with Highway 54 in Osage Beach and cuts the mileage from more than fifty miles (without the bridge) to less than five (with the bridge). This side of the lake begins at the west in Versailles (the county seat of Morgan County). This area has the historic Martin Hotel (once a stop on the 1846 stagecoach route), which houses the Historic Morgan County Museum, and a nostalgic downtown featuring unique shops, restaurants, and a circa 1930 Royal Theater. Nearby are golfing, dining, attractions, and the only completely handicap-accessible cave in Missouri. Continuing to drive south on Highway 5, you will reach Gravois Mills, the lake area's oldest town, platted in 1884. This is the headwaters area of the Gravois River that feeds into the lake. Here, you will find antique shops, quaint restaurants, and a scenic private trout hatchery that offers public fishing.

Continuing to drive south, you reach Laurie, which has the Shrine of St. Patrick Church, home of the National Shrine of Mary, mother of the church. This is a nondenominational shrine, dedicated to mothers everywhere. Off State Road O is the original St. Patrick Church, cemetery, and museum. Built in 1868, it has been carefully restored and is now listed on the National Register of Historic Places. Laurie is the small town that has about anything you might want or need. It has shopping, a multiscreen theater, golf, and nightlife and live music on and off the water. As you continue to drive south, you drive into Camden County and the communities of Sunrise Beach, Hurricane Deck, and Greenview. Lake West is the area we settled into in 1960 in the community of Sunrise Beach.

Appendix 2

In 1982 I wrote this two-page note for my dad for Father's Day. You will see how we all became lake people and how important my dad and mom were to me growing up.

Father's Day, 1982

Dear Dad,

    I hope this is a very special Father's Day for you. Let me share some of my memories which make you the best dad in the whole world.

    I remember many afternoons waiting in the driveway for the potato chip crumbs you saved just for me.

    I remember my sorrow over a lost skunk and how you proved once again to be a hero to me when you replaced him with an exact replica.

    I remember you soothing my anxiety by taking me for a walk — to the operating room.

    I remember learning to print as nice as you.

    I remember your expert swimming lessons which made many years at the lake fun.

    I remember the many triumphs and tribulations centered around the minnow tank.

    I remember being glad to be home, sitting on your lap and telling you about the fun I had in Coldwater.

    I remember your in-depth lessons on pool care and my feelings of pride when there was no dirt left after a vacuum.

    I remember the many obscure places we located hay and the hard work we put into getting it home and unloaded.

I remember my elation the Saturday Koby arrived and how you took the time to share with me and to get her pinned up temporarily.

I remember how you translated Algebra into an understandable language over many evenings on the floor.

I remember the excitement when Chiefy would try to climb the cab of the truck.

I remember my dependable bed making partner.

I remember learning to operate a stick shift while you operated the clutch.

I remember you rescuing me from my only flat tire and calmly accepting the fact I ruined the tire.

I remember your patience when I injured the boat and your perseverance when we had to be towed out of the launch position.

I remember how you shoveled out the drive to get me home from college.

I remember our trip to Lincoln, the tv. purchase, and the difficult good-by.

I remember affirming your belief a stuffed animal is all I need when a kitten arrived for Christmas.

It is obvious you have had a profound effect on me and I want to say Thank You!

Love,
Alis

Printed in the USA
CPSIA information can be obtained
at www.ICGtesting.com
LVHW091036010224
770615LV00019B/142